The Unfinished Revolution

By Al R Suarez

Table of Contents

Intro

Around the time this book was first published two great people died. First, Garcia Marquez, an author's who's work inspired me immensely, who died April 17th 2014. Then my friend and comrade Marty Droll, who died May 16th his was a young death, so tragic. And so I dedicate this book to them both. It is impossible to write this intro without first mentioning my previous book entitled "Solidarity Forever? The Struggle of an Occupier", published last year in Tampa, which consisted of a semi- autobiographical series of essays along with political commentary I wrote at the time, and added to in hindsight, to contrast my view in my post-occupy experience, drawing conclusions based on my experiences in the occupy movement as a whole. Both as a direct participant, and an outcast of that movement, as countless others became outcasts in a similar fashion, an outcast of outcasts if you will. As has been done in social movements throughout history especially in the US in particular when it is activism for justice, potential leaders are discredited or gotten rid of, but history has a way many times of the truth coming out in the end and for those vilified to be vindicated.

This, my second book, takes a different approach. Rather than rely on personal experience, it will go into the theory of revolution, and how it can be put into practice, based on the past experiences and errors of social movements in general, such as the lack of leadership, discipline or organization which contributed to the downfall of occupy, its infiltration and eventual near total destruction.

From the remnants of occupy, the civil rights movements, human rights movements, etc, this book is an attempt to fulfill the old Arab proverb "In every defeat there are seeds of victory, and in every victory there are seeds of defeat." There are indeed seeds of victory in-spite of political activism in this country and the world over being on a decline after 2012. We need only recognize them and figure out how to take better care of the garden as those seeds of revolution can help bear the fruit of real change and a new age for our children to grow up in to the triumph we deserve. For a more just and equal world, a world of humanity and progress, an ideal world. With my moving to Miramar, leaving Tampa, and pause in my studies (as my past activism was effecting me in academia this past semester), I am devoting this time to writing this book which I have had the intent of writing since the moment my last book was published, which took a year to write. I do not know how long this adventure will take me, but I am confident this book will be better than the last. It is fitting that this intro is written a day before my 2 year anniversary of my arrival back to Florida, which was when

I tried to settle back on an occupy camp in West Tampa near the ghetto, to no avail. The past two years has been dedicated to my studies, writing and activism. And I will persist in this cause wherever it takes me. As I took the train to my new home yesterday I read a biography of Malcolm X I been trying to finish, called A Life of Reinvention, indeed revolutionaries have had to reinvent themselves, and the unfinished path of revolution is upon us, us the new generation must continue this path.

In the final analysis, occupy was inspired by other movements and in great part by the Arab Spring, the Indignados then started in Spain, and eventually Occupy Wall Street came about, it spread to the nation's capitol then throughout the nation. It was a preview to revolution, a preview to what can come. It scared the hell out of the elites and the so-called government, but was ultimately crushed; however the spirit of rebellion still lives on. The anger at the injustices must be directed in the right way, if so, it can be an unstoppable force, I am a witness to that and still firmly believe the aims can be achieved, if we only unite. A new political party must be formed with the remnants of the other smaller ones to combat the two big ones in a corrupt system. This book is my humble attempt to best articulate our plan of action to replace the current system with another one. We must raise the consciousness of the people, which is already in the process of being raised, tactical retreats, non violence resistance, and other moves were made during occupy and all these acts or lack of acts can be analyzed and used to advance the cause, rather than be erased by the pages of history. The myth that the victors write history is not always the rule, we must prevent it from being so. Out of agitation, from the campuses, the youth will be the vanguard of the movement.

In Solidarity,

Al R Suarez

Miramar, Florida

April 8th

2014

Chapter 1

The Pre Revolt of Arabia & Its Historical Implications In The World Stage

I first want to start this chapter by showing a article I wrote when the protests were first starting against Mubarak in February of 2011 where I predicted he would be toppled and this would help spark revolts throughout the world:

"**Egypt: Preview To World Revolution**
February 1, 2011 at 3:37pm

3

By Al Suarez

After Egypt and the Middle East (North Africa, and possibly Asia Minor included), will not be Europe inflamed in revolution, nor Latin America will go further to revolution, it is my prediction in the next couple years the American Empire will fall and a new and better society will come about in America herself via a revolution to a eventual world revolution. A Socialistic movement towards freedom and social justice will emerge, these are exciting times indeed, my generation will be the generation of change, but not by liberal reform, but by social revolution, with social networks, and other forms of organization adapting to modern times in methods but learning from the past in the united front.

For it is with direct action on a massive scale as conditions come and are made for the new society, the new frontier is upon us, the question is when not if this new Aquarian age of Socialism can come upon us as Capitalism fades away, the State mechanisms of oppression will cease and repression will fail as the fear tactics of intimidation become inadequate for the massive inspirationist movement upon us which whether it lacks leadership or not is a truly populist movement for progress and evolving of society for the greater good of the cause.

Egyptian justice will be swift, and a ecological protectionist force will be in place to insure the survival of not just man, but of the very planet, the very air we breathe. The food crisis is a direct result of global warming and the pollution caused by man which must inevitably be fixed by man. Oppositionist forces of the current order unite for a new wave of rebellion towards the demands of our human rights with dignity, with liberty and justice for all. In essence, we must remember the notion that has always been true, we the people, divided fall, united rise, let us rise and build a new civilization, but not from brute force, but by the voluntary will of man to make a better world for our children."

If you know history you can predict many things and prepare yourself for the course of events. You cannot always be right, therefore I was wrong about the downfall of US empire quite yet, but I knew of the importance of what was going on in Egypt and its world implications. The revolt or rebellion that changed an era in the 21st century was the movement that ousted Ben Ali in Tunisia and Mubarak in Egypt in the spring of 2011 known as the "Arab Spring". Ben Ali in contrast to Ben Bella, an Algerian revolutionary who led the struggle for independence against the French, shows the anti-thesis of a leader, as more and more Tunisians realized the true nature of Ben Ali. These regions were once part of greater Arabia but constitute many different races and tribes, such as the Berber and various Bedouin tribes. Ben Ali was backed by the French, and Mubarak by the US. These movements eventually inspired the indignados movement (indignant ones) in Spain suffering from the corrupt bourgeois Socialist regime of Zapatero, and the Greek rebellions, suffering from an economic crisis that originated in New York in 2008 and finally reached Europe by 2011.

Wherever the economies were most hurt and bailouts were made to benefit the elite, such as Ireland and Portugal, rebellions in Europe sprang out. The British and German people were also upset over their government's bailout of these countries (the British bailed out the Irish, and the Germans the Greeks, both former enemies).

The origins of the rebellion in New York later that year came from the Arabs, therefore it is necessary to look at the "Arab Spring", and its consequences in the region today and much of its complex problems and history. Many in the West are unwilling to accept the Arabs could revolt on their own without an invasion or infiltration of some type from the West in toppling these regimes that the Western government had supported. These assertions were much like the myths the Egyptians were incapable of building the pyramids or the Incas Machu Pichu and they had to have help from extraterrestrials.

Ben Ali was a French puppet, Tunisia like much of Africa was an economic colony of Europe much like it was a territorial colony of France, just like Algeria and a large part of Morocco. Historically Tunisia was the epicenter of the anti Roman rebellions inspired by General Hannibal, who almost conquered Rome herself much like Attila The Hun, leaving with his army in the Western extreme of the Empire in Europe, with his army of Carthage (modern-day Tunisia) along with other allies from the Pyrenees in Spain (Hispania) arriving to the Alps of modern-day Switzerland where Germanic tribes resided, eventually Hannibal got into the Italian peninsula herself. In the end Hannibal was betrayed, defeated, the Romans returned to Carthage and burned the country to ashes, even putting salt into the ground to prevent crops from sprouting. Out of the remnants of this ancient country came about the modern Tunis.

It is no coincidence in neighboring Libya Gaddafi named one of his sons Hannibal. Libya was under the oppression of the Italians before the rise of Gaddafi, and the re-colonization of Libya before the arrival of the German Rommel to North Africa, was a primary goal of Mussolini during WWII, an attempt to make history repeat itself as it often does. Gaddafi's grandfather resisted the Italians and was killed as a result, leaving behind resentment against the Italian rulers in the Gaddafi tribe like much of Libya. After the Italians left the corrupt Libyan King was ousted by a young commander, Moamar Gaddafi, who remained in power for decades. Libya is the second largest North African country after Algeria and is situated between Algeria, Tunis and Egypt. Gaddafi considered himself a Pan-Arabist and Pan-Africanist, wanting to unite the oppressed people of the world, and for Libya to be their world stage.

The imperial plans of Italy in the 1930s and 40s before Gaddafi's time, were extended to the plans to re-colonize Ethiopia as well under the Italian flag, Ethiopia unlike Muslim Libya was a primarily Christian country which is south of Sudan, Sudan being south of Egypt, Ethiopia has an important coastline which is part of the Red Sea. As the British had control of Egypt at the time territorial disputes between the empires were not uncommon. WWII more than a war to fight fascism, was a war of empires whoever won would influence the rest of the world and have much control over its resources, as we saw the rise of the American Empire in the 1950s as the British Empire faded, and their colonies gained independence, this was culminated with the independence of India, thanks in great part to the efforts of

Mahatma Gandhi and his nonviolent movement. What's fascinating is that the rebellions in North Africa recently, were conducted primarily by non-violent tactics. The US losing its German and Japanese competitors in the post-WWII era, those countries in ruins, the US was able to advance in the car industry and many industries as it went through an economic boom as an emerging Empire.

Today the US continues to be a military super-power, however its status as an economic super-power is being called into question, especially if you consider both the European Union and Chinese's currency are worth more than dollars today. 95% of the increased income in the US from 2009-2012 went to 1% of the populace. http://blogs.wsj.com/economics/2013/09/10/some-95-of-2009-2012-income-gains-went-to-wealthiest-1/) The lack of an egalitarian economic system and the furthering of a Capitalist system with bailouts, etc, further angered large sections of the American society, who called for a movement against the 1 percent control of the economy. This culminated into the Occupy Wall Street movement in September 2011, the Wall Street bankers and elites with government accomplices, were culpable for much of the crisis including the housing crisis, and much of the youth took to the streets.

The EU had many social programs and safety nets to protect the workers and poor of their nations. However the US influence in the EU eventually resulted in the EU having a crisis much similar to that of the US, the words of Noam Chomsky rang through when he said "Europe is a junior partner of the US".

Egyptian and Libyan Socialist leaders Nasser and Gaddafi helped bring an end to the dependency on their former rulers in Britain and France and brought about an independence movement. Military alliances with the Soviet Union also helped maintain their independence as the British, French and Israelis attempted to take the Egyptian Sinai, but Einsenhower refused to intervene and the attempts were soon called off, as Egyptian tanks rolled in to defend their territory. Gaddafi called out years later the treason of Sadat as the new ruler of Egypt, in giving up on the Palestinians of Gaza in making peace with Israel in 1979, Gaddafi also had tensions with Mubarak when he took over in Egypt. As long as the North Africans remained divided, Gaddafi would be surrounded by pro imperialist leaders. Later an "Arab Spring" came after Gaddafi himself, however the authenticity of that revolt is questionable to say the least.

There can be no question however into the legitimacy of the demands of the occupiers from the Occupy Wall Street movement in the US, and this phase I call the pre-revolt, as a pre-revolutionary scenario is coming into play with the reemergence of an old tradition in the US, rebellion, as it seems to be reborn and inspired by external events as described, as well as internal conditions and a heightened awareness being contributing factors.

In essence, the pre revolt has already come, invariably the actual revolt towards a revolutionary epoch will come from the most developed country in the world, the US, which is probably also the most unequal country in the world when it comes to the nation's wealth. Built on the ashes of Native civilization and rebuilt on the backs of slaves and the exploited, the US is a country only about two centuries old, but which has a lot to offer to the world. The more developing nations have also inspired movements in the US, as mentioned North Africa, and even to an extent South America, the US has a significant amount of Latinos who are sympathetic to the democratic anti imperialist movements spreading throughout the continent such as the Venezuelan and Bolivian cases (Maduro/Morales), uniting with various governments in the region of a more populist or progressive stance than that of the US who fight to take off the shackles of US imperialism, as from within the US there are also forces fighting it's foreign policy.

Chapter 2

Revolutionary Consciousness

The most important factor in implementing any revolution is the raising of the consciousness or awareness of the masses, and inspiring them into action with revolutionary activism. Bold action but also intelligent action is necessary. The masses in the US are ripe for revolution, in poll after poll the US are overwhelming distrustful of the government (80%), more than ever in the nation's history. In one particular poll, the US people preferred cockroaches over Congress-people (http://www.npr.org/blogs/thetwo-way/2013/10/09/231015154/americans-prefer-hemorrhoids-and-cockroaches-to-congress). There is also a consensus on the distrust of mass media and its manipulation of the facts (60%) (http://www.gallup.com/poll/157589/distrust-media-hits-new-high.aspx).

The problem is not so much ignorance, but complacency, and fear, these are factors that result in the overall passivity of the people in the face of injustice. Especially of the youth who are always the vanguard of the revolt. Behavioral drugs, mandatory jail sentences, have pacified the youth, especially colored youth, as there are a simultaneous drug and class war in the country.

In Peru, Ecuador and Bolivia, the coca leaf is legal, and has medicinal purposes such as altitude sickness you can suffer in the Andes. The natives have chewed these leaves for centuries and they are also used in a tea form. In Colombia of course because of the powder form it is created into, it is illegal to purchase these leaves for they are an illegal drug. If some drugs were legalized, such as marijuana, which is already being petitioned for legalization in many states and passed in states like Colorado and Washington State, this could help end the drug war on the border in particular, where a wall is being built on the border with Mexico.

The fear and complacency must be countered not just with education, but inspiring, raising awareness and changing the discourse of the culture with a counter culture, alternative media, protest and other forms of activism. A new political party to counter the two major parties, who are one in the same, is needed, a left opposition, organized, united, taking from other 3rd parties like the Socialist or Green, must come together, anarchist, occupier, Socialist, etc.

The word anarchist like many political words originates from ancient Greece, anarcho, meaning no rulers. Democracy, democracia, means power of the people. Republic, republica, means representing the people. Direct democracy, workers councils, General Assemblies, are what are needed to bring about the common aims in a united front, balancing these different ideologies, we must replace the current system or order with another. Methods may be different, whether of the violent or non-violent struggle, but the objective of a more egalitarian society, is one that can unite the hearts and minds of people in the struggle, especially starting from the campuses and student groups, to spearhead these campaigns. Reform is nothing but a Band-Aid on a cancerous wound, to get to the root cause, we must find the root, the cure, and this can only be done through transformative revolution, starting with the consciousness of the society. The society has an anger building up that must be unleashed and directed in the right way towards revolutionary change.

The General Assembly in occupy was facilitated in the direct democracy practice. To be accepted to be financed for something by the individual donations given to occupy, you had to show you were a member of two or more working groups, when you were signed off for the working groups, you would be bought a train pass for example, to take the local train to meetings or other areas you needed in the city.

This at least was the functioning policy at Occupy Boston when I was a participant there. However, to be able to bring a block and stop a proposal at a GA (General Assembly) you only needed 10% to vote that your block was substantial. I tried to bring up reforming the block from within by giving a person the right to make a block only when being a member of two working groups, to prevent outsiders coming again and blocking a occupy proposal of controversy, such as the level 3 sex offenders ban which banned certain groups of people from attending our meetings.

Direct actions (DA) were done outside the authority of the GA. The black bloc new wave Anarchist groups used to claim not to be hierarchy, but go and do direct actions that sometimes backfired, such as the destruction of property under the banner of occupy non-violence and in front of cameras. The contradictions and lack of leadership, resulted in confusion, and even though consciousness was raised, it was not enough to bring a revolutionary change to the conditions on the ground, whether in the occupy camp or the areas the occupiers wanted to make a difference, whether in a poor or highly populated area of the city. To an extent, even in more rural areas occupy had a presence.

Any revolutionary movement must have the participation of not just students or workers, but the peasants, from the countryside a revolt can also be formed, such as the Appalachian people, who have been abandoned and forgotten throughout the years. All outcasts must be cast into the revolutionary movement, most Americans, especially the youth, do not vote, and this voter bloc can be used to back the new party, so much so it would be hard to rig any elections whether national or local.

Again, the alternative media, whether radio, TV, or book, must be used to expand the message of non-conformity and revolt throughout the country. We must be prepared to defend ourselves as we are fighting the establishment and all its power. We do however outnumber the elites can with unity and organization can lead the country on a different path. Leaders are first going to receive attempts to discredit them, then possibly blackmail, then worse, political assassination. However all this can be prevented by uniting, division will always be taken advantage of by external forces, the divide and conquer tactic that goes back to Julius Caesar himself in how he divided Celts and Germanics along the Rhine, and then went on to conquer Britannia.

We must focus also on adapting to the modern lingo and ways to be relatable to the masses. Using old words like "bourgeois" when talking to average people would cause confusion. However, there is a mentality of the upper Middle Class who want to be rich that being rich is good, by any means. This mentality can even be reached to an extent in the pipedreams of the poor who still hold on to the American Dream which is nothing but a myth today. Even Jesus said the rich do not get into heaven, Jesus kicked the moneychangers out of the temple, liberation theology is a revolutionary forced to be reckoned with, strong in countries like Paraguay, here in the US there is a significant amount of people of this thinking. Even the new Pope, a former Jesuit, is bringing about a more progressive approach in the religious doctrine.

We must however not be a copy or a model of another nation's revolution, they can help inspire us to conduct one in our own fashion in the US, and with a democratic force that can counter the current order of things. The New World Order is in fact the Old World Order, the elites across the globe have maintained their control and divided us, a new world needs to come about. But not a world of obedient order, as the anarchists like to rebel against, but a world where we are free to express ourselves and reach a more egalitarian society, not of war or aggression, but of peace, cooperation and progress. Not all forms of competition are bad either, but fair play would be needed in the new society, with an effort to get rid of monopoly control of markets or enterprise.

Chapter 3

The Role of Socialism *In* The New Society

Socialism is an economic and political system based on workers' rights, workers democracy, towards an egalitarian system based on the principles of social justice. More and more Americans in this crisis are open to alternative forms of government, and Socialism seems to be on the rise worldwide, if we see what's going on in South America especially. The natural resources of the people, especially oil, in particular in Venezuela, are being used to make social programs to protect the poor, and ultimately, end poverty, as is the legacy of Hugo Chavez.

If we look at the history of Socialism, we see post-Soviet Union the old guard of Stalinist bureaucrats, and the Trotskyists, battling it out in sects struggling to regain influence in the revolutionary movement. Rather than limiting ourselves to labels and sects, the left needs to unite behind the banner of social justice and combat the disease of Capitalism and all its symptoms, imperialism, racism, fascism, poverty, homelessness, crime, etc.

Socialism still has a role in such a movement, but it must be clearly defined and old divisions must end to accomplish common goals. To conceptualize, realize and actualize the revolution, we must not just analyze the conditions or wait for the conditions, but make the conditions ready to bring about the struggle for social change in the political and economic realm. A revolution of love, and values, as we are one human family, is a strong revolution with a moral force. In the end the ends do not justify the means, we must have the moral high-ground when facing the enemy of elites and all their pawns whether the police or some other force to be reckoned with.

The military have oath-keepers who are ready and willing to prevent martial law in conjunction with the Constitution. In Russia we saw with the royal guard, the Cossacks, they changed sides with the people against the Czar and this was a fundamental shift that brought the inevitable downfall of the Czarist regime in favor of the Bolsheviks. To see all military or police as "pawns of the 1 percent" and therefore your enemy, your ignoring the fact they are of working class backgrounds in a majority too, and are afraid of losing their pensions, not being able to provide for their family, etc, and are coerced into the frontlines against their own people.

Guilt and the realization of their self-destructive path can help them actually become allies. Such as the turn of the Egyptian military against Mubarak. You can argue the Egyptians are not much better off with Sisi, but how much longer will he be in power? Morsi was not in power for that long. Soon the Egyptians will find a reliable leader who can stay in power and implement the fulfilling of the demands of Tahrir Square for the freedom and independence of the Arab people, and this would spread as the people would unite and not let their natural resources be exploited by the West for cheap prices by corrupt and "pro-Western" governments.

Chapter 4

The Importance of Anger

You cannot write about revolution without mentioning the factor of anger and how it can be directed and attribute to a revolution full of courage and justice for the common men and women of the society. A revolution is not just educational or about activism, it is spiritual, a spiritual force that is based on the releasing of anger do to injustice. No revolutionary can exist without having suffered or witnessed injustice. The words of Che Guevara come to mind "If you cringe with indignation at every injustice, then you are a comrade of mine." Indeed, to Che it did not matter so much your political ideology, if you were against the injustice of imperialism, you were his comrade in the struggle for justice.

Che drove with his friend Alberto Granados on a motorcycle throughout South America witnessing poverty and much injustice which was his first transformation as a revolutionary, we know from his cherished motorcycle diaries. He later supported the government of Arbenz in Guatemala before it was toppled by a US backed coup, by the late 1950s Che in Mexico banded with a group of Cuban guerrillas who embarked on a voyage that would end in January 1959 with the triumphant entry into Havana with the dictator Batista fleeing Cuba. The example and sacrifice of Che in Bolivia in 1967, has made people associate revolution with his face, and rightly so. However the myth of Che is one thing and the real Che is another.

Those who have suffered the most injustice will lead the revolution. The Native Americans, such as the Seminoles here in Florida, who never signed a treaty with the US government like the other tribes, can be a force to be reckoned with. Many of the elites from their tribes have joined the Capitalist system and for tax breaks on their reservations and control to Casinos, given up any claims for land or independence in their autonomous territories. There was a time runaway blacks and Seminoles united in Florida against the US invasion when the Spanish left, and intermingled and formed their own race and nation.

This part of history has in large part been forgotten as people are divided along racial lines, in the ghetto, the ghettos that the government invented just like the gangs and drugs used there. It was expressly the wish of Jefferson for Florida to be "taken from the Spanish" to go after runaway slaves and to attack the Indians that protected them. While Louisiana was purchased by Napoleon who needed money to keep up his military campaigns, the Spanish Crown was weak and the new American statesmen wanted to take that land, as the British had tried in the past. At one point out of Saint Augustine, the Spanish almost successfully conquered Savannah in southern Georgia which they were going to call upper Florida.

The word ghetto originates from Venice and the Jews that were forced to live in communities there. If a Jew left the ghetto they would have to wear a red hat and many times they were spat on and beat up for simply being Jews. Shakespeare even made a play about this era. We later heard this term in the ghettos set up by the Nazis where Jews were stationed before being sent to the concentration camp, such as the Warsaw Ghetto, which is known for being the spot where the Jews smuggled in weapons and resisted the Nazi occupiers in Poland.

The poor living in ghettos, the Native or indigenous people living in reservations, they are the ones that need to unite and demand that their rights be given to them in the new society, so their voices can be heard. When their anger is done and solutions to their problems are made, a new and peaceful society can come about.

We see in northern Europe today such as in Germany and Scandinavia, the economies are still intact while the rest of Europe is practically suffering. Many immigrants in Europe from North Africa, South

America, and other regions, are returning to their countries and are better off for it. Why is northern Europe still intact? The "nanny state" or state with strong social programs to help people get back to work, are in these countries, the southern European region tends to have weaker programs, and people are still out of work. Therefore, in the new society we must have strong programs, but also encourage people not to depend on government handouts as we see is common in the ghetto, where the youth resort to delinquency to get back, because of the lack of jobs or opportunities.

Chapter 5

Tactics

Is non-violence an effective tactic anymore? When the media ignores or misrepresents a movement, and there is still a significant amount of the populace who pay attention to this media, what is the point of sacrificing one's life in the face of brutal violence, when there can be no effective way to go about it, the people will not back you, and you will be isolated, imprisoned, injured or dead? This is an ongoing debate that originates in the US back to the days of Martin Luther King and Malcolm X. Malcolm and King essentially wanted a society where the rights of the black man in America would be respected. Both were leaders in organizations, both transformed and reinvented themselves. King was first exclusively for civil rights, then he became part of the peace movement speaking out against the Vietnam war. He was also for labor rights, and eventually was for human rights altogether much like Malcolm.

Malcolm as part of the Nation of Islam was for the supremacy of the black race, he grew overtime to step away from this thinking and his affiliation with the "Black Muslims" and started a more secular group and embraced Orthodox Islam. Malcolm instead wanted to work with African and Arab nations allied with him to go through the UN and condemn the US practices of genocide and discrimination against black people in the country.

This is something Malcolm could have united with MLK on as he reconciled with King and other civil rights leaders, however Malcolm was assassinated before this unity could be brought about. King over the years after Malcolm's death before his own assassination, became more radical and expressed his pride in being black. When King could not be controlled, blackmailed or discredited by the government, he choose like many leaders in history, to die for his cause, both Malcolm and King knew that death was near, but continued in their cause.

The question of tactics is quite divisive and controversial, but is one we continue to tackle. I firmly believe in self-defense and do not find that violent, offensive violence from an aggressor is inherently violent and is to be expected by those the revolutionaries oppose as has been the case through-out history. At the same time as there are defensive measures, it is more symbolic to perform a massive boycott and non cooperation with the system that can bring the system to its knees as the system depends on us.

Civil disobedience goes beyond passive resistance, and such measures are aggressive but not violent in the face of the enemy. Defiance and other inspiring acts can make the difference, such as the mass arrest of activists on the Brooklyn Bridge during Occupy Wall Street, that was a turning point in the movement and got a lot of people behind it, although the surge in the movement was temporary.

Again leadership is essential for the movement to survive and internal drama not divide the movement till it ceases to exist or has lost its base or foundation to continue as a menace to the current system. Leadership must be backed by a disciplined organization, a leader without organization is like a navy captain without their boat. One must work with the other in harmony in carrying out the tasks.

Chapter 6

The Crisis of Leadership

What is a leader? What is a false prophet? What are the characteristics of a true leader, and that of a false prophet? What are the red flags that show a cult of personality around a false prophet is being brought about, and how can this persona be countered? These are the ultimate questions we face when we decide to take part in a movement where leadership is essential to the revolutionary cause, for the cause needs a champion to bring it about, and to fight to keep it going. Occupy fundamentally was a contradiction as the slogan "We are all leaders, and none of us are leaders." Was repeated in our heads. Whenever anyone came to the occupy camps and asked who was in charge, the answer no one, always caused confusion.

There needed to be in the GA process leaders elected to represent us. The excuse that if that happened we would be infiltrated made no sense, since we were so easily infiltrated for not having leaders to protect us from disruptive agent provocateurs that are always sent into such movements and caused much paranoia and division.

A real leader is one who inspires others into action by putting themselves on the front-lines, they are the ones to make the first step and in little regard for their own safety, is ready and willing to make the ultimate sacrifice. The false prophet is the opportunist who is neutral during a moral crisis, who stays in the sidelines and in the opportune moment comes out as a leader, but who will send others out to a risky task rather than put themselves in harm's way.

A false prophet makes their own philosophy and makes a heretic or discredits those who do not follow their philosophy. A false prophet exaggerates their importance and takes credit for things they should

not take credit for. If you experience a false prophet the best way to deal with them is a frontal attack out in the open from the beginning before this false prophet acquires too much power and can harm you. Those around the false prophet must be warned and the false prophet must be on the defensive and justify their authority, if they cannot justify their role as leader must be taken away and given to someone more suitable, as that person can be voted in through a process of a council or General Assembly democratically among the group or organization you are a part of.

The workers council in Russia during the revolution of 1917 were called Soviets, and the Soviet Union initially was to represent the workers democracy espoused by these organizations who worked underground for decades during the tyrannical regime of the Russian Czar. Leaders in these groups before the civil war and ultimate blockade on the Russian people, were bold and intelligent. To prevent a false prophet a "Stalin" or "Napoleon" if you will, there needs to be unity and clarity in the message of the party or organization you will be a part of.

Chapter 7

What The New Society Will Look Like And How The United Front Will Divide Up Their Roles

Inevitably, the new society can only come about through a united front, some compromise will have to be made. As always history can show us past mistakes to apply to the present for a better future. A good example is the Spanish Civil War of the 1930s. International brigades of anti fascists banded together and fought on the frontlines of Aragon, Catalonia, and other parts of the Iberian peninsula of Spain. They had to make compromises at the time between anarchists, Socialists, Trotskyists, libertarians (although libertarian has a different meaning in the US), etc.

All had commonalities but differences. Many debated over agrarian reform should be carried out in the lands that they controlled, or whether any changes at all should be made while the war was going on. A good literary source for this time in history is George Orwell's nonfictional work "Homage To Catalonia" which details his role in the POUM militia, which was also a political party, that consisted of various factions of anti-fascists as mentioned, who banded together, before the Stalinist betrayal and the return of the bourgeoisie to Barcelona along with the "national front" which resulted in the fascist victory and Stalin making a pact with Hitler, as Hitler supported Franco in Spain who was ultimately victorious in 1939.

No matter the compromises we must never give up on our principles or betray our fellow comrades when the new society is formed, it shall only be the beginning not the end. As Che entered Havana victorious in 1959, it was only the beginning for him, as an internationalist, the revolution would bring him to fight in the Congo in Africa and later in Bolivia in the center of his native South America. The

euphoria of a victory or triumph can weaken the senses and help bring about the cult of personality, as we see to this day a Castro is in power in Havana. Vigilance is needed.

To divide up the roles the best of the libertarians in the new society would be in charge of protecting the civil liberties in the nation. Often we see in the current system the very people who are supposed to protect our rights are finding way to violate them and cover it up with the law. As the law is void of justice and must be disobeyed. The Socialists would be in charge of the economy, making sure wealth is distributed fairly and equally to protect the workers, eventually the role of the State would wither away and people would take charge of their destinies in the community.

The anarchist in essence, would be in charge of the nation's security. For they better than anyone else know that authority needs to justify itself and that it cannot be abused. With this combination of forces for good, am sure the new society can progress and a better future can come for our children. For the remaining 10 pages of the book am going to fill it with articles of mine for the final chapter.

Chapter 8

The New Society (Articles)

The Betrayal of the Venezuelan Students, And The Counter Revolution in Venezuela
February 20, 2014 at 12:47am

By Al Suarez

At the risk of losing friends am going to tell the truth of what I know on Venezuela based on the reports from my comrades on the ground. I started working on this article earlier today but because of technical problems had to rewrite it. I find it is about time to write an article on this topic. Students started protests on the streets of Venezuela for two principal reasons. Corruption, and deliquency. However much of the delinquency today is coming from their own counter-parts. I sympathize with some of the students who are used as pawns and manipulated, thinking what they will do will not harm Venezuela. I myself have been in protests for years and was arrested a couple times during occupy protests, which I subsequently wrote a book about for our modern history.

We must understand the historical context of how this conflict has risen, and the crisis it has resulted in from these events. To call these protests peaceful one would have to be delusional, it

would be hard putting a camera on the protests and ignore the dozens of molotov cocktails being thrown at Venezuelan police in the Ukrainian fashion. But Venezuela is not Ukraine. Nor do I think Venezuela will go into a civil war in the Syrian fashion. As an investigative journalist (unlike propagandist journalists who just do sound-bites, especially in US media) I must ask, what are the reasons behind the protests? Who benefits? The reasons could go back to the original coup attempt against Chavez himself in April 2002, or to the municipal elections in Venezuela in December last year.

Most who are familiar with the Venezuelan case know of the relationship of Maduro with Chavez, that he is trying to maintain Chavez's legacy. A legacy of progress, of 21st Socialism, including Christian and Bolivarian Socialism, in a democratic and revolutionary way. We must also understand the personas of Leopoldo Lopez and Henrique Capriles.

First let us look at the municipal elections from two months ago that happened throughout the provinces of Venezuela, which were a reaffirmation of Maduro's popularity, 60% voting in favor of his party the Socialist Unity Party, as Maduro won the presidency against all odds against Capriles who was a veteran at presidential elections having tried to run against Chavez multiple times, and who only ever won the governorship of Miranda province, which he lost in the municipal elections of December 2013. We see even one of the main leaders of the opposition in 2013 lost in those elections, and the Venezuelan electoral system is impeccable as confirmed by countless international observers, here is what Jimmy Carter said about Venezuela, who heads the Carter Center who supervise elections all over the world "If only the US had an electoral system as good as Venezuela." I found it amusing and commented on this on the radio when

Secretary Kerry said that he was not sure whether to accept Maduro's victory, when Kerry himself on a smaller margin accepted he lost to Bush. That was back when I was still blind and young and supported the democrats in 2004. Soon after that I became an independent leaning towards 3rd parties.

So we see time and again the right opposition in Venezuela when they take part in fair elections end up on the losing side. Was it not predictable these sore losers would resort to these methods "inspired" by Ukraine and other violent protesters? Is this not a counter revolution and a betrayal of Chavez's legacy, these students calling for a foreign intervention, or worse an invasion from the Yankees to the North themselves? What if the roles were reversed, what if rich students, like many of those in Venezuela, from Harvard, where Leopoldo went, or from Yale, called for the Chinese to invade the US and for Obama to be assassinated, what would happen to these students? And if they were arrested, would it be called a human rights abuse?

In the final analysis, the American Empire would after all be the most beneficial in an unstable Venezuela, which is full of rich oil that the imperialists are dying to get their hands on again for the elites or 1% to continue in their control of the region. Only time will tell. I think Venezuelans are waking up and smelling the Coffee, so is the rest of Latin America, and we in the US need to as well. Our so-called government loves to meddle in other nation's affairs while ignoring the

NSA spying and other injustices that have been exposed these past few months, how convenient for them, but us the real journalists will keep them in check.

The Presence of Socialism In America: Will 2014 Be The Year For Social Revolutionary Change?

January 6th 2014

By Al Suarez

Social Security, Workers Comp, Unemployment, Minimum Wage, Disability, Food Stamps, Weekend Off, Vacation Time, Children Not in Workplace, Women in the Workplace, all these things exist in America because of Socialism, Socialism can never work in America? It already does. And if America needs anything its more Socialism. We are being attacked by an unprecedented menace to our rights as working class people and students by a corporate capitalist system bent on taking away the few bread crumbs of rights we have left in this "democracy", either with the credit system of debt and wage slavery, or with the brute force of those brave activists who take to the streets to demand these rights. True democracy can only be reached through Socialism, we must not be afraid to say this, third parties must unite, a left opposition friends and comrades, must be formed to oppose the other two parties who even Obama admitted recently have little difference between the two!

A spiritual and intellectual revolution is on the way, true social change can and will be made, so I invite you to be the first to start to read the passages of a new book I am working on to be published this year, which will be edited by Comrade Marty, which will be called "The Unfinished Revolution" which will be sort of a part II to my last book which describes my experience in the occupy movement and our failure to carry out the revolution our ancestors over 2 centuries ago carried out from Boston, Philadelphia and other historical cities of revolution.

The legacy of Hugo Chavez who perished last year is still alive in the hearts of rebellion against American empire of our Latin brothers and sisters to the south. These are the last days of empires and imperialism, here at home we must do something about it. Anarchists, Libertarians, Socialists, Humanists, let us unite! Now is the time to for action, not just words, for words without action is like a car without gasoline. The fire of revolution is upon us, we may differ on methods, but our aims are the same, the new society is upon us! Leadership, discipline and organization are the three keys to any social movement without these qualities any movement is doomed to failure. Egalitarian democracy can only be achieved through making in America a new political party and joining forces with all the 3rd parties and independents with the common aims, and making this into a movement who will use non violence, boycotts, strikes and other means to keep up the fight, the struggle continues, la luta continua... Down with fascism! Down with the police state!

In the final analysis, those that negate Socialism exists or try to portray us as monsters, they do not see the reality or ignore the reality and maintain the illusion that democracy exists as Orwell says. We must defy the current order of things and bring about a new consciousness, a new program, to the people, to the masses of hungry and homeless, to the poor and vulnerable, we must offer them a way out, before complete chaos becomes us...

My Speech & Testimony Given on October 19th 2013 at "2013 World Women Court on Poverty"

I first would like to say what a honor it is to be here before you on this historic occasion. I drove 20 hours with Bruce and others to get here from Tampa and so far its been worth it. In particular, yesterday's testimonies struck me, I thought I had a hard life, but they went through hell and back. But my story should not be compared to anyone's. I really became a activist in Elementary School, at the age of 11 or 12. A lady helped me write a article when I lived in Vermont that was published in the Brattleboro Reformer Newspaper, Brattleboro was like a city in the area of southern Vermont, but was more like a big town. I had moved at the age of 6 from my native

Boston, am proud to be from the city where the American Revolution was born. I was born on October 1st 1984, 1984 also happens to be the title of a book of one of my heroes, George Orwell. Am proud to speak to you from the city of brotherly love, where the Declaration of Independence was written. Anyway it must have been 1995 or 96' when I was going to Putney Central School in Vermont. The name of the article in the Reformer was something like "Bullying at Public Central School", where I interviewed students on the bullying problem, which I was also a victim of. Parents were pressuring the school administration on their strict bullying policy, when the school laid up, the bullying got even worse.

Since then I have had the grace to know what I want to be, a journalist. Journalism is activism. Orwell said "Journalism is printing something someone else does not want printed, everything else, is public relations." Yesterday the question why was asked many times. It reminded me of a quote from the Archbishop of Brazil "When I fed the poor, they called me a saint, when I asked why they were poor, I was called a Communist." Indeed, whether its the war on Communism, Drugs, Terror, they are all ultimately a attack on the most vulnerable, the poor. We are not ashamed to call ourselves poor, we are a symptom of a disease, a cancer, a severe ailment, called capitalism, which is corporatism, and ultimately, fascism. Homelessness is the worst of these symptoms. Dr. Stein (Jill Stein, 12' US presidential Green Party Candidate and member of jury) knows a real doctor tries to find the cure, to radically find the root cause to problems and diseases. I have come to realize we are not in a democracy, we are a in a corporatocracy, or to be more precise, CEOcracy, where the average CEO to the worker in the US gets 600 times more, no thanks to the bailouts, while in countries like France its 30 to 1.

Back to my story. I went to my first protest at the age of 17 to protest the Afghan War, I went to Burlington Vermont and was quoted in the paper there. By 2011 I lived abroad, and had a different perspective coming back to my country. I went to live with my father for a couple years to Peru, as well as Spain. My father a US citizen of Peruvian origin, who has 2 Masters from Harvard, has had to leave the US many times to find work throughout my life because of discrimination, this has also helped inspire me to be an activist. In 2011 shortly before the occupy movement started in the US, the worst day of my life, September 2nd, my little sister, my only sibling, Natasha, who I adored, passed away. At the time I lived in Georgia with my mom and stepdad, and I tried as best I could to reconcile with them, I was worried for Natasha's daughter, my niece, 3 at the time, and subsequently was kicked out, where I became homeless on the evening of October 12th, 2011. Bruce by then was already occupying DC. I took a greyhound to Vermont then and saw my niece, by November I was living on camp at Occupy Burlington Vermont. After a few weeks a camper apparently shot himself in the tent, he died, and our camp was shutdown. I then went to Occupy Boston, where I had my first occupy arrest defending camp. I also went to Occupy Savannah, Occupy Providence, Occupy DC, Occupy Tampa, Occupy Tallahassee and Occupy New Haven, which I wrote a book about a couple months ago.

Am now back in College, and am the president of the Domestic Violence Awareness Club at my campus. My sister was a victim of domestic violence, this was kept from me till after she died, there has still not be justice for Natasha, it helps me to help people. Am doing well, living with my father in Tampa. What happened to me made me stronger, wiser, when your down you know who your real friends are. The best occupiers were the homeless occupiers, since they had nothing to lose, especially the colored occupiers, but they became scapegoats in the movement, a dying movement which was inspired by movements in Europe and the Arab World. We must learn from what happened it has made me a better man, we must fight selfishness with selflessness, and build a better society! We need revolution, not reform, we need to discuss methods, beyond dialogue, to bring about real change! The conditions to revolt are there, we need only recognize them. Am going to stay in this country and fight for our rights, for a better world for our children, thank you!

The Government "Shutdown" Is A Symptom of Capitalism

October 9th 2013

By Al Suarez

Every 15 years or so in the Capitalist enclave of the US, where the dominant power are the corporate Capitalist class, predictably there is a crisis or shutdown of the economic and political system. The infantile question of "who started" the shutdown should not be our focus, but what we are going to do about it, should be the question. The cancer of capital and all its forces has a symptomatic or systematic problem, whether its homelessness, poverty, economic inequality, political exclusion, isolation, abandonment, selfishness, chauvinism, racism, all these reflect the Capitalist culture which must be combated with a counter culture towards the ideal society, one of sharing, loving, and caring for one another as a society bringing about a social movement of progress.

The occupy movement must be defined in our modern history as a peaceful attempt at revolution, from October 2011 in DC, the movement spread, originating in New York, the non violent activism had its modern roots in the Arab Spring movements such as in Tunisia and Egypt, which quickly spread to the Greek and Spanish protesters suffering economic decline in Europe. The failure to acquire fundamental change in our society in this attempt, as occupy was crushed by brute force of the State, means we must adapt tactics? Like any doctor, when there is a disease or ailment, the root case must be found in order for it to be cured. Fear, apathy, hate, ignorance, these are all the early stage symptoms of Capitalism, which cannot coincide in a real Democracy or even Republic.

Che Guevara started in the guerrilla force which embarked on Cuba, as a medic, therefore he was a doctor, he later joined the fight as a revolutionary, but he continued to see the diseases of imperialism, and Capitalism, in all its forms, as a sickness that needed to be fought and cured with a counter ideology, such as Socialism, the method being, revolutionary struggle by violent means, which does not work in many cases, as we see MLK and Gandhi were more effective using non violence and getting public opinion behind their morally just causes, such as independence, self-determination, human and civil rights.

Nevertheless, today marks the 46th anniversary of the untimely death of Che Guevara, who was executed in a school in a Bolivian village on orders from the American Empire in Washington. It is rightly so to talk of him on this day in relation to his legacy and influence in rebellions throughout the world such as the resistance against military invasions, like in Vietnam, and the struggle we see in Syria today, where a proxy war is being waged against Assad. Rather than delve into the divisive controversy of Syria, let us speak on issues we can find common ground on, fundamental justice for example.

In the final analysis, the US is a society that is for lack of a better phrase, a Corporatocracy, or to be more precise, CEOcracy, the average CEO's salary to a worker in the US in the latest figures I know, as it grew fast with the bailouts, is 600 times more, while in countries like France its just 30 times more. The gross economic inequality is not something that needs to be fixed, the system needs to be transformed, this cannot come about with reform, but only with revolutionary change, can the masses of struggling students and workers take back their government. If tyrants backed by the West like Ben Ali and Hosni Mubarak, can be overthrown, than anything is possible. A quote comes to mind "Do the impossible, be a realist."-Che Guevara Sounds like a contradiction but Che believed you could do impossible things and still be a realist, a realist optimist you could say.

The True Nature of Internationalism: The Unity I Saw From The Left Forum Among Greeks & Turks In The Struggle

June 11th 2013

By Al Suarez

On the 7th of June commenced the historic Left Forum in Manhattan, NYC, at Pace University. Such distinguished people such as Noam Chomsky and Oliver Stone came to speak. Also the VP of Bolivia came to speak in the end but I missed that. There was talk of Cornel West coming but never saw him. I was able to speak with both Finkelstein and Sherry Wolf before they debated each other which I was able to take photos of and will probably discuss in a separate article. But probably the greatest experience of all was with my Turkish and Greek comrades in Zuccotti Park on the 8th, this event lasted 3 days, but the event on the 8th really struck a cord with me, after we marched from the Left Forum I was able to see a unity that almost brought me to tears. What I could imagine it was like for those Greeks and Turks to be together as one. After a meeting on the fascist dangers in Greece, we left the meeting with the more diehard comrades who went forth to march to show solidarity with Turkish comrades at their invitation. Someone needed to help hold the sign to lead the marchers, and of course I volunteered, wearing my kaffiyeh (Arab scarf) proudly, we marched forth. All the division of centuries was forgotten as I marched with about 50 Greek comrades towards Zuccotti Park with signs as we gave a new chant for the city to hear: "Istanbul, Athens, NYC, resist in every ciiity!". Over 1000 Turks remained at Zuccotti Park, where the occupy movement started, waiting for us, who had been protesting all day as they returned to that park to show solidarity with their people protesting in Istanbul, Ankara, and throughout Asia Minor, the Anatolian spirit was something to be admired.

Ataturk was a nationalist but he helped end the tyranny of the Ottomans. He took in exiles like Trotsky, even helped some Jews during WWII, which historically the Turks had done if you look at the exiled Jews from Spain. On my mother's side I have Jewish roots and it was a emotional thing for me to see this unity that governments had fought so hard to prevent. Divisions that go back all the way to Alexander The Great, the man I was named after. And many of the Turks present were internationalists and were overjoyed at our arrival to the park. I felt like someone from a scene of Lawrence of Arabia arriving victorious at some bedouin camp in the desert. Only what surrounded us were skyscrapers. I expected for them to barely take notice of us, but they applauded overwhelmingly as we came, as they parted so we could enter the park. I decided for a comrade and me holding the sign that said We Are All Greeks, to stand up on a bench and show the sign to the world, which got the crowd going even more.

Finally we moved to where the speakers, both a Greek and Turkish woman, would speak, who's videos I will provide below. I felt it was a historical moment, something I could tell my grandkids someday, and it happened where occupy started, a movement I was deeply part of. With people giving Peoples Mic, which you can see in the video, repeating what the person says since the cops won't let a loud speaker. Today we have people in tents like it was in Egypt only in Turkey, and we must show solidarity with them being arm and arm with our comrades in the struggle the world over, and let the resistance come back to the US! For our children! And the children of our children!! Let this example of unity and internationalism never be forgotten!

https://www.facebook.com/photo.php?v=583231961700092

http://www.youtube.com/watch?feature=player_embedded&v=rmZBs3CGCHo

My Hero Is Dead

March 6th 2013

By Al Suarez

Comandante Chavez was a man defamed by much of the world media, from fear from the establishment, like all great leaders. When the defamation stopped working it is possible the CIA had him poisoned causing him the cancer, as many relatively young heads of state in Latin America who allied with Chavez had suddenly got cancer, and the CIA has been known to use this tactic, Chavez himself suggested this possibility. One of the most common insults towards Chavez, which caused me much indignation, was that of dictator. Would a dictator allow free speech? In Venezuela opposition TV which dominated the channels as they broadcast from Miami and other cities, called for Chavez's assassination every day and Chavez tolerated it for free speech of "journalism", if Fox News tomorrow called for the killing of Obama, you think those reporters would not be in jail? This same propaganda has circulated rumors that Chavez was in a coma when he was still well enough to write letters to the public while he was sick with cancer.

I asked Professor Chomsky what he thought it meant for Latin America the death of Chavez yesterday, and he said its hard to predict. I think Chomsky is wrong. Chomsky was a old friend of Chavez, a man who is much older than Chavez, I think whats predictable is there will not be civil war but the Venezuelans will unite for the sake of Chavez and his sacrifice for his people. Chavez was not a Venezuelan leader, he was not a Latin American leader, he was a world leader, and history should remember him as so.

I know what it is to lose someone close, I know what Chavez's daughters are going through, the suffering of his people yes, but imagine his daughters, his grandchildren, in these moments. Chavez was not known as a intellectual but was well read. From poets like Galeano and Neruda, to intellectuals like Chomsky, Chavez knew literature well, and applied it to his philosophy. We will continue in his legacy, that of rebelling against the injustice of imperialism wherever we can find it, and trying to make a difference in this world. Chavez was able to continue Allende's legacy, the first democratically elected Socialist, the Chilean revolutionary who was taken from power and took his own life on the other 911, but in 1973.

Latin America unite now more than ever in honor of Chavez! Do not let the bourgeoisie divide you!

Chavez made me proud to be a man, proud to be Latin, and proud to be a anti imperialist. He was the father of us all. Chavez's faults only made us love him more it reminded us he is human like us and he was the first to recognize his faults. Chavez did so much to unite the Latins and Arabs under the banner of anti imperialism with the inshallah-ojala unity (the words for hopefully or godwilling in Arabic and Spanish, which are similar), men like him in history are unique and precious. Life is so unfair life was taken from Chavez before he could enjoy the inauguration he fought so hard to earn from his reelection. Chavez helped in the negotiations with the FARC rebels when Green Party presidential candidate Ingrid Betancourt of Colombia was being held by them, upon her release she went to Venezuela to pay homage to Chavez. Chavez even used Venezuelan gas, CITGO, to help poor families in the US.

A great man died yesterday, let us not let his death be in vain. Chavez was able to return to his country before he died, as countless Latin American leaders in history have died in exile including Simon Bolivar, who helped liberate much of Latin America and the Caribbean from the Spanish imperialists. Today we have the imperialists here in the USA, and Chavez and his legacy of leaders in South America from Correa, to Morales, to Humala, etc, will continue. I hope to return to South America soon, as a journalist, and revolutionary. I do not worship a hero but I admire a hero, a man, who like all men and women had his faults, but one unique in his role in history, over a decade in power, he left a Venezuela on their feet with dignity not willing to give their natural resources to empire any longer. Long live Chavez!! Long live the BOLIVARIAN REVOLUTION FROM VENEZUELA TO ALL OF LATIN AMERICA!

Al Suarez founder of Americans For Chavez

1 Year Anniversary of My Return to Tampa: What Has Happened & What Has Not Happened

April 9th 2013

By Al Suarez

I dedicate this note to my sister who I had a dream with this morning, may she rest in peace, and may her daughter continue her legacy.

After the Occupy New Haven civil war where I was considered a homeless occupier leader, as being homeless was a crime by the "normal occupiers" which was brutal and caused me much physical and emotional distress to say the least, I returned to Tampa, naive, convinced that, the demons would not follow me there, but all was planned before I arrived on camp in West Tampa, to have me kicked out, put on the street, left to die, for if it was not for a cousin who took me in, that is probably what would have happened as I was once again betrayed by my "allies" who on April 10th, stopped defending me or did not show up to General Assembly. Or in other words, a Witch-trial was set up, against me, where gangs of people were brought many having never met me or talked to me but already with the intent to vote me out and get me out, at all costs.

This all started when on the last day of January 2012, I arrived in West Tampa, where I stayed till mid February when I had to go to court in Boston for defending this movement. All during that time I got along with everyone on camp. From Boston I went to New Haven, where I stayed for almost 2 months. The end part of my stay is when all hell broke lose on that camp, the tensions were there before I even arrived, it would have happened either way as it did on many of the remaining camps. It did not matter that I was arrested twice for the movement and had been a exemplary activist during and well before occupy. I was to be the villain, the hero no more, as was the case of many of us. Many of these people were prisoners sent by the State to stir trouble on camp, some were on probation and part of their deal was to spy on us or disrupt us. To my shame some were drug addicts sent by shelters, but most of us homeless at that time were real activists, diehard in fact, with nothing to lose. Many non homeless occupiers were drug induced and paranoid as it was. Accusation of cop or rapist was the norm. But I wont get into New Haven. That is a chapter in a book I am writing. The topic is Tampa. What has happened, or failed to happen, in my activism in this community thanks to accusations from provocateurs is what I will get into.

Two dear friends & comrades were still able to stay with me during the RNC protests (Republican National Convention) in August last year. Sparro, a woman who did face painting at Occupy Wall Street, where it all started, who was with me in New Haven, and the other, Bil, a man I knew as the facilitator of Occupy Boston who stayed on in GA (General Assembly) long after most of the people left the movement, fed up with the drama and infighting. From April to July 2012 I stayed with my cousin, and tried my best to recuperate spiritually from the injustices that were done to me, to regain my strength and continue the cause. I was very lucky, he even had a bedroom available for me, and I had a netbook computer working with internet use near by. I cannot complain. I am eternally grateful to him for this. I stayed there in Brandon, Fl, till I was finally able to acquire the money to get a place here in Ybor City, the Latin Quarter of Tampa, where I wanted to live for some time. So as planned, in-spite of all the attempts to stop me, by the RNC I was able to house activists, so many people put the word out it was a "FBI set up" to "entrap" activists, that it was a fake "safehouse", the amount of paranoia in these words, and the amount of people who believed it were incredible. Even after I spoke in favor of occupy at city council they continued their campaign of defamation against me. They contacted local businesses where I frequented in Ybor, and stopped at nothing to sabotage every aspect of my life. If they could have taken the food stamps I used to eat they would have. What hatred, what anger, was this based on insanity, or greed? Or both? I dont know, but these people only instilled in me a will to live in Tampa more, to defy their resistance to my existence, like the Palestinians would say.

You see this is not a subject I touch much on, since its "divisive", but its the anniversary today, so this will be on my mind. And I am only touching on bits and pieces as this is a complex issue. Do I consider myself a occupier? Yes but the original occupier, from September 2011, not what remains, with a few exceptions like Bil, of the movement. Destruction of property, and not non violence which I promote, is the common tactic of "anarchists" who remain with occupy. My book is called "Solidarity Forever? The Struggle of an Occupier", a struggle indeed, and where is the solidarity today when so many people can get away with attacking a fellow comrade who wanted nothing more to fight for the rights of those oppressed in this society, whether women, minorities, children or whoever needed to be fought for, and the world over for the future, for love, for true activism? They almost destroyed me, destroyed it all, but I learned, and this helped make me stronger and make my character stronger, so thank you! I continue to fight for homeless in the Tampa Bay area, and those who attacked me here have backed off because perhaps it has got in their thick skulls I am a devoted activist! And attacking me will ONLY make them look bad! From the example of my father and others I have learned to be determined, to bring my life together, and also to continue activism, a sacred cause to me, for real peaceful revolution in my lifetime.

www.ingramcontent.com/pod-product-compliance
Lightning Source LLC
Chambersburg PA
CBHW080359290526
45791CB00009BA/2924